BULLSHIT

EVERYWHERE

fuck.

fuck.

fuck.

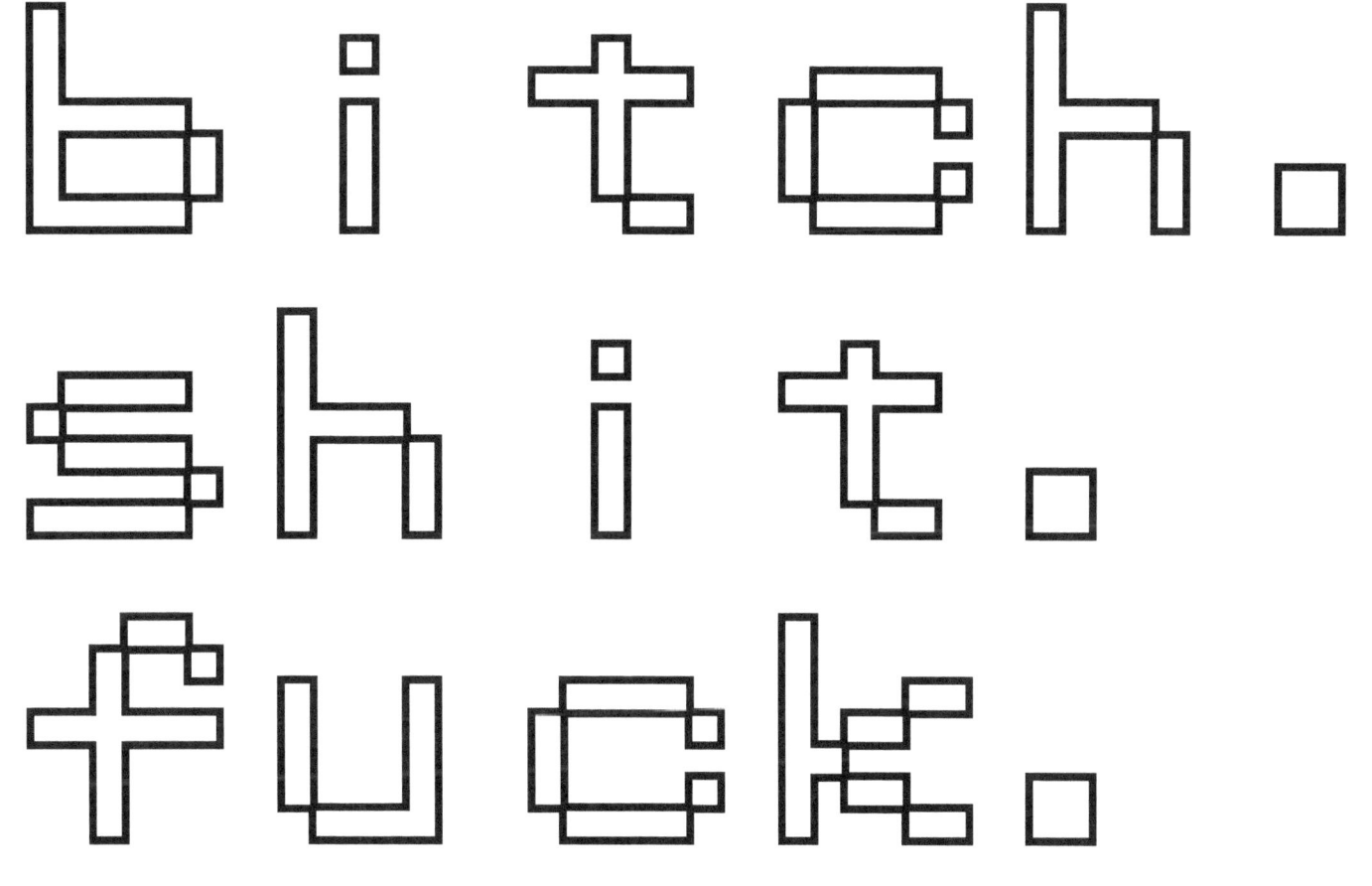

bitch.
shit.
fuck.

CUMGUZZLER

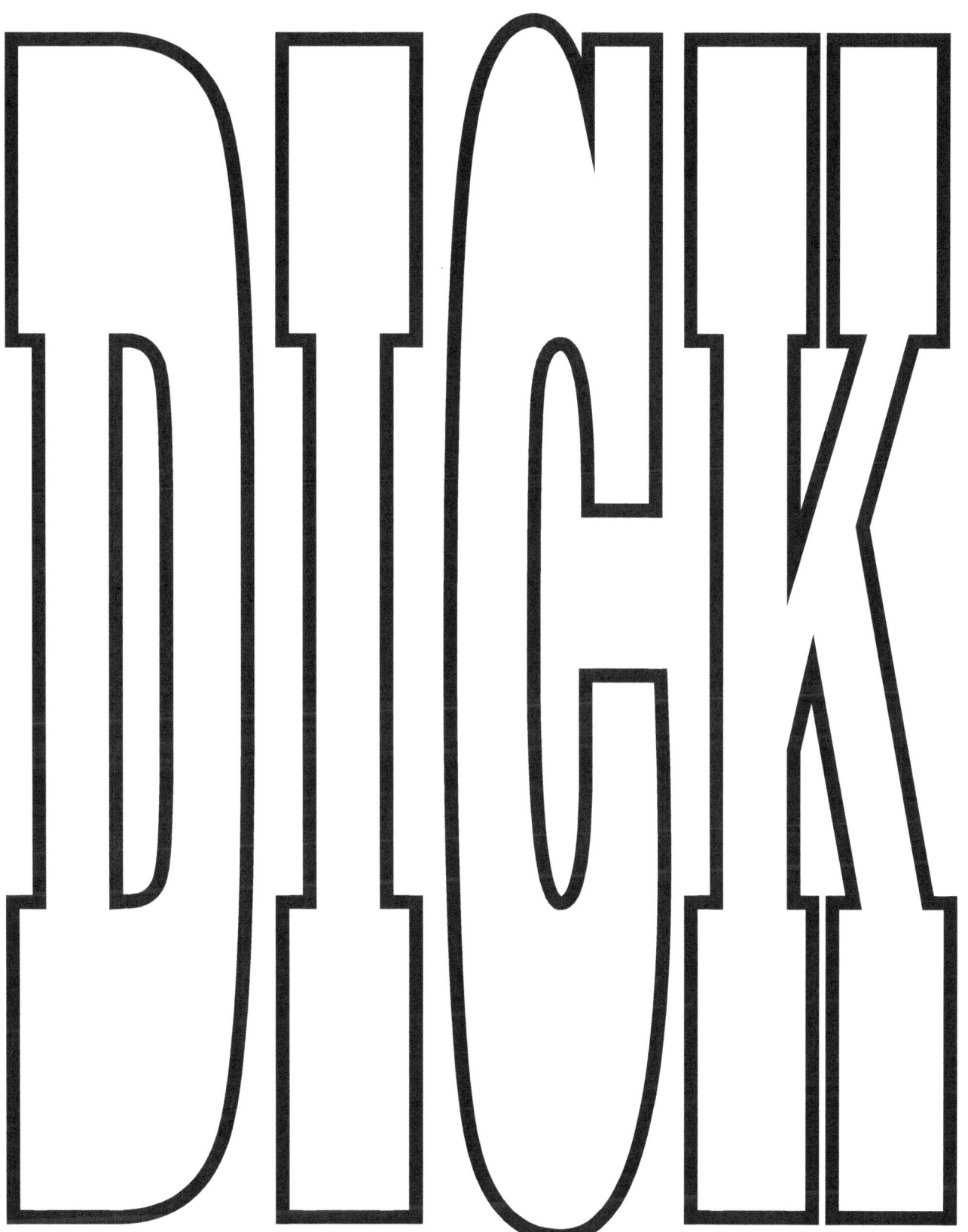

λ λ λ λ

S S S S

S S S S

h h h h

ο ο ο ο

ι ι ι ι

є є є є

GO FUCK YOURSELF

KEEP ON
FUCKIN'

PUSSY

KISS MY ASS

LET THERE BE SHIT

NUTSACK

ASSHAT

RIMJOBBING

FUCKFACE

DILDO

SWALLOWING

CLITSUCKING

DICKRIDING

BUMBLEFUCK

SHITBALLS
FUCKHEAD
COCKSUCKER
ASSHOLE

Stupid

Shithead

Dickriding

Slut

www.ingramcontent.com/pod-product-compliance
Lightning Source LLC
Chambersburg PA
CBHW082015230526
45468CB00022B/2295